HOW OUR BODIES WORK

The SKELETON and MOVEMENT

JACQUELINE DINEEN

Editorial planning
Philip Steele

M
MACMILLAN

First published 1988
Reprinted 1989

Published by
MACMILLAN EDUCATION LTD
Houndmills, Basingstoke, Hampshire RG21 2XS
and London
Companies and representatives
throughout the world

Designed and produced by BLA Publishing Limited,
East Grinstead, Sussex, England.

Also in LONDON · HONG KONG · TAIPEI · SINGAPORE · NEW YORK

A Ling Kee Company

Illustrations by David Anstey; Sallie Alane Reason, Val Sassoon/Linden Artists and Linda Thursby/Linden Artists
Colour origination by Chris Willock Reproductions
Printed in Hong Kong

British Library Cataloguing in Publication Data

Dineen, Jacqueline
  The skeleton and movement. — (How our
  bodies work). — (Macmillan world library)
  1. Human mechanics — Juvenile literature
  2. Man — Attitude and movement — Juvenile
  literature
  I. Title ,   II. Steele, Philip   III. Series
  612'.76   QP301

ISBN 0–333–45962–8

Photographic credits

t = top b = bottom l = left r = right

cover: Trevor Hill

6t Ann Ronan Picture Library; 6b Frank Lane Picture Agency; 7 Ann Ronan Picture Library; 11l, 11r Vision International; 15t, 15b Sporting Pictures; 16 Vision International; 19, 21t S. and R. Greenhill; 21b Sporting Pictures; 23, 24 S.and R. Greenhill; 25, 26, 28 Vision International; 29l Science Photo Library; 29r, 30t Trevor Hill; 30b St Bartholomew's Hospital; 31, 32 Vision International; 33t, 33b Science Photo Library; 34 Barnaby's Picture Library; 35t Trevor Hill; 35b Science Photo Library; 36 St Bartholomew's Hospital; 37t S. and R. Greenhill; 37b Vision International; 40t D. C. Thompson; 40b Trevor Hill; 41 The Hutchison Library; 42t, 42b Sporting Pictures; 44 Vision International; 45t S. and R. Greenhill; 45b Science Photo Library

---

Note to the reader
In this book there are some words in the text which are printed in **bold** type. This shows that the word is listed in the glossary on page 46. The glossary gives a brief explanation of words which may be new to you.

Contents

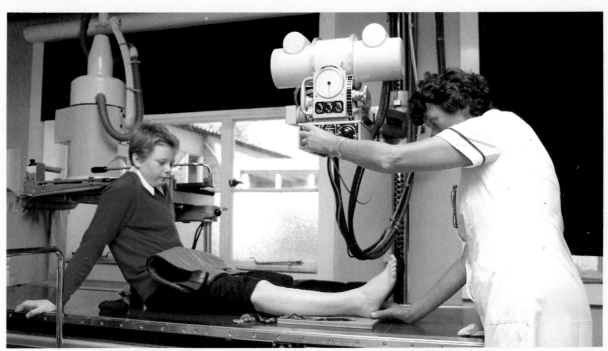

Introduction

▼ All creatures need to support their bodies in some way. The soft body of the jellyfish is supported by the water in which it floats. The crab's soft body is held together by a hard outer casing of shell. Birds, like humans, have skeletons inside their bodies.

cormorant

jellyfish

crab

What happens to a tent if you take away the frame underneath? The tent falls down. The human body is made like a tent. The skin and flesh is supported on a framework of bones called the **skeleton**. Without the skeleton, the body would collapse.

Humans, birds, reptiles and fish all have a line of bones down their backs. This backbone, or **spine**, supports the rest of the skeleton. All animals with backbones are called **vertebrates**. Insects, shellfish and jellyfish are **invertebrates**. They do not have a backbone. Some invertebrates, such as snails and crabs, have an outside casing or shell. A jellyfish does not have a skeleton or a shell. Its whole body is soft.

Underneath the skin

If you press your skin, you can usually feel bone underneath. Bones are hard and strong. The skeleton protects soft parts of the body, like the heart. The heart is surrounded by bones so that it cannot be bruised or pierced.

Bones are not dry and brittle. They are living, growing things. The outer layer of a bone is hard and rigid. Inside, there is a soft, fatty substance. Your bones grow bigger until you are an adult. If a bone breaks, new bone grows to join the pieces together again.

All your bones are linked together. At the places where they join, there are pads like cushions. These pads are called **cartilage**. Cartilage stops bones from rubbing together and wearing away.

Your skeleton could not move without **muscles**. Muscles are made of a stretchy material which is attached to the bones. Muscles can shorten and pull the bones with them.

Finding out about movement

The human body is like a very complex machine except that it can move far more smoothly than a machine. How does this happen?

This book is about the skeleton and how it works. It describes the different bones and muscles and what they are made of. It also explains the things that can go wrong with bones and muscles, and what you can do to keep your bones and muscles healthy.

▼ Skeletons not only support and protect the body, they also help it move. Human beings can make many complicated movements. They can run, walk, jump and pick things up.

Bones and muscles
work together
to make us move.

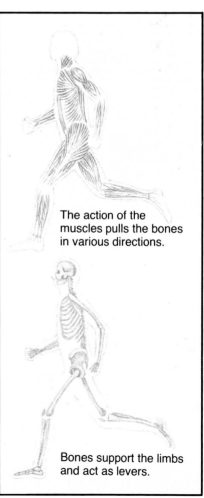

The action of the muscles pulls the bones in various directions.

Bones support the limbs and act as levers.

Learning about the body

For thousands of years, people did not understand how their bodies worked. They were too afraid of evil spirits to find out. In ancient times, people believed that evil spirits in the body caused disease and death. Some people believed that bones could be used to make magic spells.

Gradually, people began to learn about bones. They could feel their own bones inside their flesh. They could see bones inside the bodies of animals and people that were killed.

▲ People first learned about bones by trying to mend broken limbs. They found that broken bones grow together again. Here, strips of wood are being bound to the patient's leg. These kept the leg straight so that it could mend properly.

◄ Once people had found out how the skeleton worked, they still did not understand what made it move. Luigi Galvani carried out experiments with dead frogs. He found that electricity could make the muscles of a frog twitch. Was this the secret of movement?

Broken bones

People found that bones can break. Sometimes they broke when they fell over or when they were fighting. People tried to protect themselves when they were fighting. Soldiers did this by wearing armour and helmets, but bones were still broken in battle.

People made medicines from plants. They gave wounded people these mixtures to drink to stop the pain. They tied broken arms or legs to straight pieces of wood to hold the bones in place. Bones did not always mend well this way. People often ended up with crooked bones. Sometimes they could not walk again.

The age of science

Much later people began to learn about the parts of the body and how they fit together. About 400 years ago, a Belgian named Vesalius wrote about how the body works. This was the first book about the **anatomy** of the human body. The Italian painter, Leonardo da Vinci, studied the muscles in the body so that he could make the people that he painted look more real.

However, people still did not understand how movement worked. What made muscles move? Two hundred years ago, an Italian scientist, Luigi Galvani, noticed that electricity from a machine made the legs of a dead frog twitch. He thought that a live frog must use the same kind of power as the machine. He believed that some sort of electricity inside the frog's body must make the muscles move.

Many years later, scientists found that the **brain** controls the rest of the body. Tiny threads called **nerves** are found all over the body. They join together with the brain to make up the **nervous system** which carries messages between the muscles and the brain. The messages tell the muscles to tighten or relax, and this makes the body move. Later, a British doctor, called Charles Sherrington, also discovered how groups of muscles work together to make the body move smoothly.

▼ People are on the move most of the time. The first photographs and films made it much easier for scientists to study movement. For the first time they could look at each tiny movement and see how the muscles and bones worked together.

The skeleton

All your bones are linked together to form the framework for your body. The bones of the head are called the **skull**. The brain is protected by this helmet of smooth, curved bone.

The skull sits on top of the spine. Run your fingers down your spine. You can feel that it is made up of small bones linked together. The narrow column of the spine runs down between and behind the hips. At the hips wide curved bones stick out on each side. These bones are joined together to make up the **pelvis**. The leg bones fit into the pelvis.

At the top of the spine are the shoulder bones, which are linked to the arm bones. Twelve bones curve around from each side of the spine to the front of the chest. These bones are the **ribs**. They form a strong cage that protects the heart and lungs.

What are bones made of?

All living things are made of millions of tiny parts called **cells**. Bone cells are one type of the many cells that make up your body.

Bones are hard but they are also light. The hard, tough outer layer is very thin. Underneath this layer, there is a mass of spongy bone. Blood flows to the bone cells through small channels inside this spongy bone. Blood leaves **calcium phosphate** in the bone cells. Calcium phosphate is the food we need to keep muscles and bones healthy. The calcium phosphate is stored in the bone cells and makes the bones hard and strong.

In the middle of your large bones, there is a red, fatty substance. This is **marrow**, where blood cells are made.

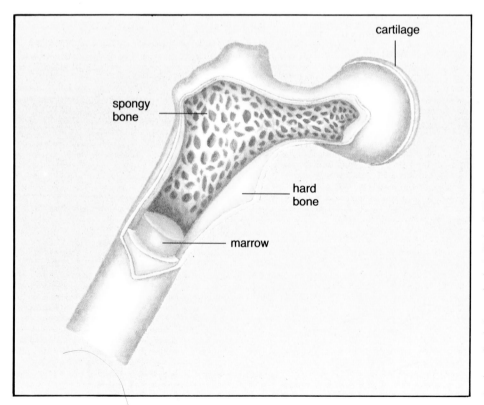

cartilage

spongy bone

hard bone

marrow

◄ The outer layer of a bone is hard. This protects the light, spongy bone inside. At the centre of the bone is fatty marrow. Our blood contains white cells, which fight disease, and red cells, which carry goodness from the air we breathe around our bodies. Bone marrow is a factory for our red blood cells.

How many bones?

A baby has more than 300 bones, but an adult only has 206! What happens to the extra bones? We do not lose them. As we grow older, some of the smaller bones join together to form larger bones.

All our bones have names. The largest bone in the body is the **femur,** or thigh bone. It is about 50 centimetres long in a person who is 1.8 metres tall. The smallest bone is the **stirrup.** It is inside the ear, and is only 2.5 millimetres long. We have long bones in our arms and legs, and short bones in our wrists and ankles.

◄ The skeleton is a living framework for the body. The bones have blood and nerves in them. We can feel pain in our bones, and they can grow and change.

▼ Some of our bones are very large and some are very small. Deep inside the ear are three tiny bones called the hammer, stirrup and anvil. They pass on sounds from the outer ear to a nerve which sends signals to the brain. Compare the size of the stirrup bone to the point of the pencil.

The skeleton

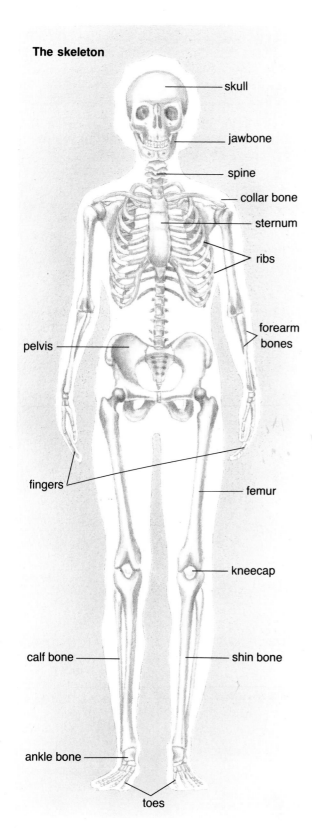

- skull
- jawbone
- spine
- collar bone
- sternum
- ribs
- forearm bones
- pelvis
- fingers
- femur
- kneecap
- calf bone
- shin bone
- ankle bone
- toes

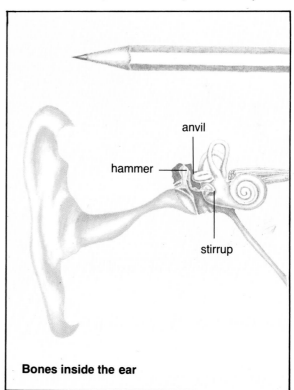

anvil
hammer
stirrup

Bones inside the ear

How we move

You cannot run forever. If you run as fast as you can, you soon get tired and have to stop. You puff and pant, and your muscles refuse to do any more work. Muscles need fuel to work. The fuel they use is a gas called oxygen. We breathe in oxygen from the air. The oxygen passes to the lungs and then into the blood. The heart pumps this blood and oxygen round the body to the muscle cells. The muscle cells contain a sugar called **glucose**. When the blood gets to the muscles, the oxygen mixes with the glucose to produce **energy**. This energy makes your muscles work. When you run fast, you pant. The lungs are drawing in extra oxygen for the muscles. If the muscles do not get enough oxygen they get tired.

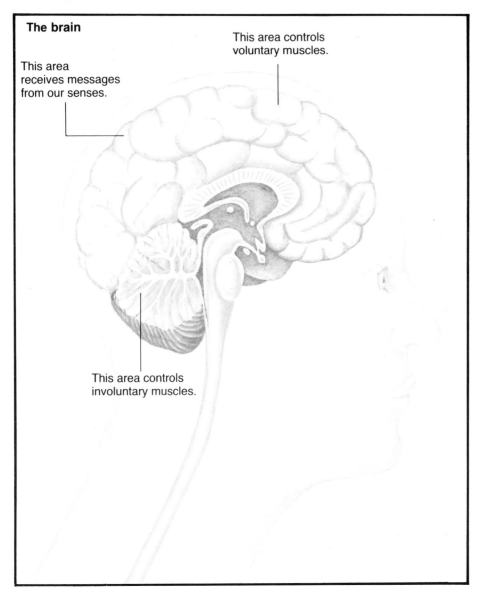

The brain

This area receives messages from our senses.

This area controls voluntary muscles.

This area controls involuntary muscles.

◄ The inside of the brain controls everything we think, feel or do. The brain picks up messages from different parts of the body and decides how the body should react. Different parts of the brain are used for different purposes.

▲ When we eat a meal, we have to think about chewing and swallowing the food. After that, the involuntary muscles take over. They automatically squeeze the food through the tubes in our bodies.

▲ These children cannot skip automatically. They have to think about what they are doing. Their brains decide on skipping movements, and pass messages along nerves to the arm and legs.

Remote control

Suppose you decide to lift your arm. How does this message get to your muscles?

Your brain controls everything you do. It is a complex group of special cells inside your skull. The brain is linked to the rest of the body by the nerves. The nerves are a bit like telephone lines. Nerve cells called **neurons** send messages to and from the brain. Thin threads of nerves, called nerve fibres, start at the brain, run down the spine and branch out to every part of the body. Your brain sends a message along the nerves to the muscles. The ends of the neurons touch the muscles. When the signal from the brain reaches the muscles, they tighten or relax to cause movement.

Kinds of movement

There are different types of muscles. Different sets of nerves control these two types of muscles.

One group of muscles only works when you tell them to. They are called **voluntary** muscles. The arm muscles and thigh muscles are all voluntary muscles. You use them when you decide to lift a glass of water or walk across a room.

The second group are called **involuntary** muscles. They keep your body working. You do not even think about making them work. For example, tiny muscles in your eyes make you blink. This keeps your eyes moist and clean. When you eat a meal, involuntary muscles push food to parts of your body where it is broken down.

Body connections

Bones do not bend but our bodies are not stiff. We can walk, bend, or stretch because of the way our bones fit together. The skeleton has joints. Joints are places where two bones meet. We are able to move and bend only because of our joints.

Moving joints

Bones do not need to move in the same way. Some joints allow more movement than others. The hips and shoulders are **ball-and-socket joints**. One bone has a rounded end like a ball. The other bone has a cup-shaped dip or socket. The ball rolls in the hollow socket at the end of the other bone. The bones can move in almost any direction.

The joints in the elbows, knees, fingers and toes are called **hinge joints**. They work like a door hinge. The body parts with hinge joints bend only in one direction. They cannot move much from side to side.

The wrists, ankles, and part of the spine have **gliding joints**. The bones slide against each other. **Pivot joints** in the neck allow the head to turn and nod.

The joints get a great deal of use so they need protection. If the bones rubbed together they would soon wear away. A layer of cartilage between the bones keeps them from grinding against each other. Strong bands called **ligaments** hold the bones firmly in place.

Each joint also has a thin lining or **membrane** around it. This membrane makes a liquid which helps the bones to slide, like oiling a bicycle so that it will work well.

▼ The bones of the skeleton are joined in various ways. Ball-and-socket joints can move in any direction. Hinge joints can only move backwards and forwards. Gliding joints can bend and swivel. Ligaments control the amount of movement made by the joints.

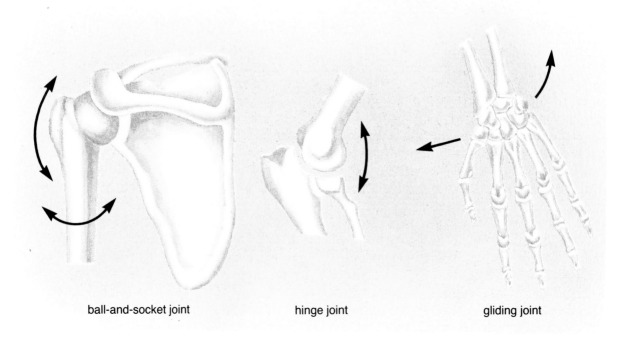

ball-and-socket joint   hinge joint   gliding joint

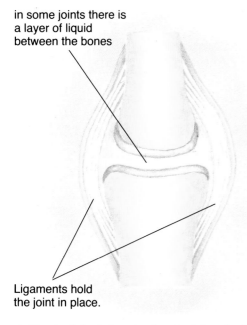

in some joints there is a layer of liquid between the bones

Ligaments hold the joint in place.

▲ **Most of the joints in the skeleton look like this. They are tied together with tough but supple ligaments. Some are protected by a thin layer of liquid to stop them rubbing together.**

▼ **The joints between the bones of the spine are cushioned by pads of cartilage. These act like the shock absorbers of a car.**

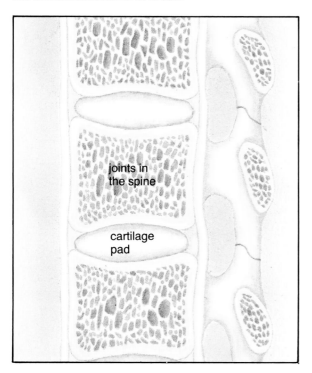

joints in the spine

cartilage pad

Stiff joints

There are 28 stiff joints in the body. Some of them cannot move at all. The lower part of the jaw is the only part of the skull which moves. It moves up and down on joints in front of the ears. The other bones in the skull are fixed firmly together by **fibrous joints**. There are joints between all the small bones in the backbone, to spine, but you cannot bend each joint separately. Each joint only moves a tiny bit. If you add all this movement together, you get a bendy column. So you can bend or twist your whole spine quite a lot.

Imagine all the little bones in your spine rattling and jolting as you walk along. This would be very uncomfortable. Each bone rests on a pad of soft cartilage. The bones press on these pads instead of on each other.

▼ **The flat bones of the skull are joined together with tough joints of fibre. These joints do not allow any movement.**

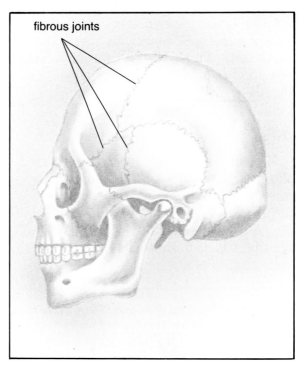

fibrous joints

Muscle power

Your body is never completely still. Even when you are asleep, you are breathing. Sometimes you roll over in your sleep, or move an arm or a leg. When you are awake, you run, jump and talk. Your bones cannot move on their own. Your whole skeleton is covered by muscles. They are what make your bones move.

Muscles make up one-third of the body's weight. The muscles are made up of bundles of very thin fibres. They are attached to the bones by tough, strong cords called **tendons**. How do muscles work? The fibres can only move one way. They can only get shorter. So muscles have to work in pairs or groups.

Let us suppose you want to bend your arm at the elbow. A muscle called the biceps at the front of your upper arm shortens and pulls the arm up. Now you want to straighten your arm. The biceps cannot make itself longer, so how do you move your arm again? The muscle relaxes and another muscle, called the triceps, at the back of your upper arm shortens. This pulls the arm down.

Pushing and pulling

Your muscles do not have to work hard all the time. If you stroll along, your leg muscles only have a little work to do. A few of the muscle fibres become shorter. However, if you run as fast as you can, all the fibres have to shorten to push and pull your legs.

▶ **All our movements are controlled by muscles. The muscle fibres shorten so that we can make a movement. To reverse that movement, another muscle shortens and the first muscle relaxes.**

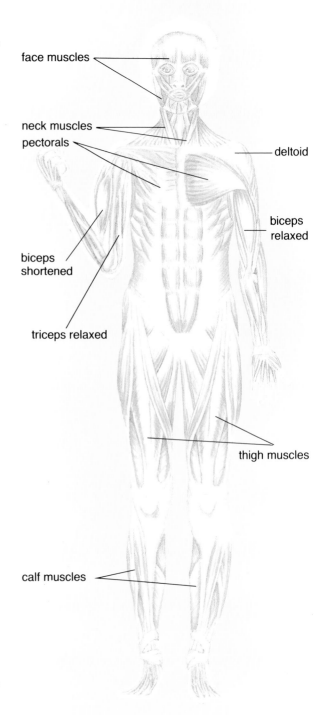

face muscles

neck muscles

pectorals

deltoid

biceps shortened

triceps relaxed

biceps relaxed

thigh muscles

calf muscles

There are over 620 muscles in the human body. Like your bones they all have names. For example, the shoulder muscles are called deltoids. The chest muscles are called pectorals.

What do all these muscles do? The face muscles are used for things like talking, chewing, smiling and frowning. The neck muscles move the head. The pectorals and deltoids lift and pull the arms. The arm muscles bend and straighten the arm. The stomach muscles control the upper part of the body. The thigh muscles raise and lower the legs. The calf muscles are between the knees and the ankles. They control the ankles and feet.

The movements of the face are made by many tiny muscles. You use about 14 of these tiny muscles when you smile!

▲ When a tennis player serves, the whole body is tense. Biceps and triceps are used to bend and straighten the arm. Shoulder and chest muscles raise the arms high. Calf and thigh muscles keep the body balanced.

◀ Biceps bulge as two strong men take part in a arm-wrestling contest. Each is trying to force the arm of the other downwards. The one whose hand touches the pad at the side is the loser.

The skull

The skull has 29 bones. Eight of these bones fit together to make a smooth shape like a bowl. This is the **cranium**. The brain sits safely inside this bowl of bone. The bones of the cranium are thin and curved. When a baby is born, you can feel gaps between the bones of the baby's cranium. The bones are apart to allow for rapid brain growth. Fibrous joints form between the bones when a baby is about 15 months old. The bones of the face and the inner ear make up the front of the skull.

◄ The cranium is shaped like a crash helmet. It protects the brain from damage. However, if we break the bones of the skull we can be very seriously injured. People who enjoy dangerous sports such as scrambling and mountaineering wear a helmet as an extra layer of protection.

The cranium is made up of eight curved bones which are rigid. The bones of the face do not move, except for the lower jaw. The joints of the lower jaw are just in front of the ears. You move the jaw when you talk, laugh, yawn, drink or eat.

This is a cross-section of the head. You can see how the bones form a box to protect the brain. Holes in the skull allow blood vessels and nerves to reach the brain. Other gaps allow us to see, breathe, hear and eat.

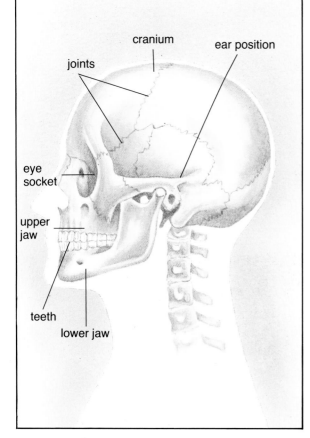

cranium

ear position

joints

eye socket

upper jaw

teeth

lower jaw

cranium

brain

nose cavity

mouth

hard palate

tongue

spine

Holes in the head

Brain cells must have oxygen and food all the time. Blood vessels carry oxygen and glucose to the brain cells. If the blood supply stops, the brain cannot give messages to the nerves.

Blood vessels reach the brain through holes in the bottom part of the skull. Nerves pass through a hole at the back of the skull. The nerves link the brain with other parts of the body. Those nerves which reach your feet are very long!

The front of the skull is not solid bone. There are holes for your eyes, nose and mouth. The eyes sit in two holes called the eye sockets. You breathe through your nose. The shape of your nose is built up from cartilage which never hardens into solid bone.

Your mouth has two bones. These are the upper and lower jawbones. When you open or close your mouth, you only move the lower jawbone. Your teeth have roots which hold the teeth onto the jawbones. The roof of your mouth is made of bone too. This is called the **hard palate**. When you talk, your tongue touches the hard palate and teeth to form sounds.

The backbone

The backbone or spine of an adult is about 70 centimetres long. The backbone takes a lot of strain. It has to hold the body upright. It is supported by the shoulders at the top and by the pelvis at the bottom. It is also supported by a lot of muscles.

A chain of bones

The backbone is made up of 26 small bones called **vertebrae**. Seven of these support the skull. The top vertebra is called the atlas. The second is called the axis. The 12 pairs of ribs join up at the back to 12 vertebrae. The next five support the back muscles. After these come five vertebrae which are fixed firmly together. These form the part of the pelvis called the sacrum.

The last four vertebrae are called the coccyx. They are also fixed together. Millions of years ago, we were animals with tails. The coccyx is all we have left of a tail! The vertebrae of the sacrum and the coccyx have not joined up in a child's spine. This means that a child has 33 separate vertebrae.

The road from the brain

Each vertebra has a hole in the middle. These holes form a channel through the spine. The bundle of nerves making up the **spinal cord** runs through this channel.

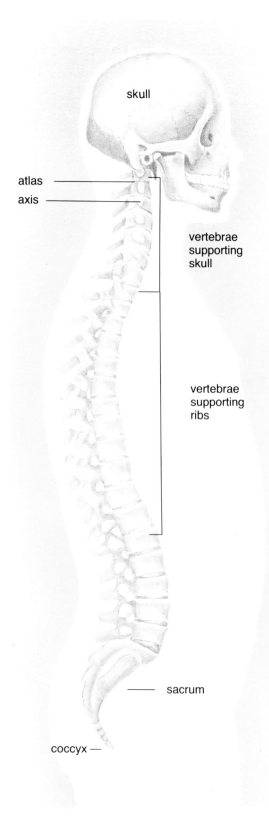

▶ The backbone or spine is a column of jointed vertebrae. It curves in a gentle S-shape. It locks into the skull and the pelvis, and so supports the whole skeleton.

The spinal cord starts at the **brain stem** which is at the base of the brain. It passes through a hole at the back of the skull and runs down the middle of the backbone. The spinal cord is the nerve centre of the body. It is made of the same material as the brain. The **grey matter** receives messages from the nerves and sends out orders to the muscles. The **white matter** sends messages to and from the brain.

Thirty-one pairs of nerves branch off the spinal cord. These nerves run to every part of the body. They control all of our movements and senses.

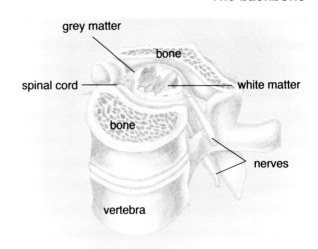

grey matter
bone
spinal cord
white matter
bone
nerves
vertebra

▲ The brain stem is the top end of the spinal cord. Messages from the brain travel down the spinal cord. You can see how the cord is protected by the bony ring of the vertebra.

◄ The spinal cord is rather like a motorway. Messages travel along it, to and from the brain. Just as small roads branch off into parts of the city, so nerves branch off into various parts of the body.

The chest and shoulders

The chest area of the body is called the **thorax**. It is made up of the heart and lungs inside the rib cage. The heart pumps blood round the body. The lungs draw in oxygen. We cannot survive without blood and oxygen. The heart and lungs are so important that they need the very special bone protection given by the ribs.

The upper ribs are joined to the **sternum** at the front of the chest. The lower ribs are shorter than the rest. They curve upwards and are joined to each other by cartilage. The twelfth pair of ribs are the shortest of all. They are only joined at the spine. These are called floating ribs.

When you breathe, you use a strong muscle called the **diaphragm**. This is a sheet of muscle across the bottom of the rib cage. When you breathe in, the diaphragm tightens and pulls down. Other chest muscles pull the ribs upwards and outwards. This gives the lungs plenty of room to fill with air. When you breathe out, the muscles relax. The diaphragm pops up, like a spring. The rib cage moves down and in. Air is squeezed out.

The thorax

- clavicle
- air to lungs from mouth
- clavicle
- shoulder blade
- sternum
- ribs
- inside of lung
- heart
- rib muscles
- covering of lung
- diaphragm

◄ The thorax contains the body's life-support systems. The ribs form a strong cage to protect the heart and lungs.

► Rugby players from Australia and Wales push against each other, shoulder-to-shoulder in a set scrum. The muscles and bones of the shoulders are very strong.

The shoulders

The shoulders support the top of the body. At the back, you have two large, flat bones called shoulder blades. Can you feel two long thin bones at the front? They join the top of the rib cage to the shoulders. These bones are your clavicles or collarbones. They are called the collarbones because the collar of a shirt or blouse lies on them. The arms are joined to the shoulders by ball-and-socket joints.

The back and shoulders are covered with strong muscles. The muscles in the shoulders control the movements of your arms. You can lift your arms above your head. The ball-and-socket joints also allow you to twist, swing and swivel your arms. When you lift or carry something heavy, the muscles in your back and shoulders take the strain.

The shoulder muscles also help to support the head and neck. The back muscles support the spine and keep you standing straight.

▲ We use the strong muscles of the shoulder and back to lift and carry heavy weights. We must learn to carry things in the correct way if we are to avoid injuring our backs.

The pelvis

▼ The big, curved bones of the pelvis form a basin for the waste system and for the uterus in women. The pelvis also supports the lower part of the backbone. The pelvis is joined to the backbone at the sacrum. The femur bones link the thighs to the pelvis.

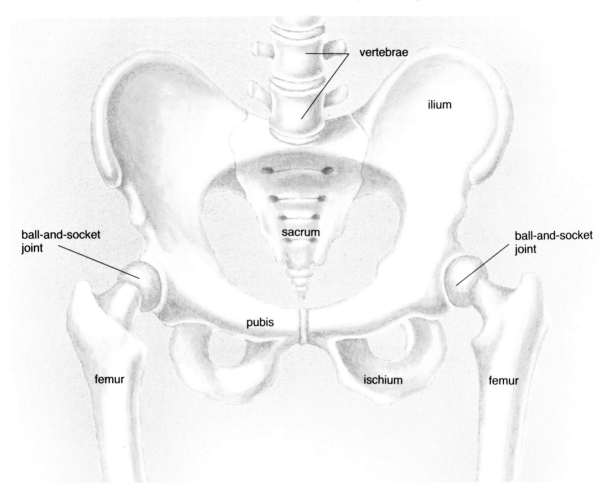

vertebrae

ilium

ball-and-socket joint

ball-and-socket joint

sacrum

pubis

femur

ischium

femur

The pelvis supports the bottom of the spine. It protects the soft parts in the lower half of the body. The bones of the legs are linked to the pelvis by ball-and-socket joints.

The pelvis is shaped like a basin which juts out at the sides to form the part we call our hips. In fact, the word 'pelvis' is the Latin word for basin. The pelvis is made up of several bones. They are all joined together and cannot move alone. The sacrum joins the pelvis to the rest of the

spine. The other bones are called the ilium, the ischium and the pubis.

At the back of the pelvis are the buttocks. They are fatty and form a pad for you to sit on. The muscles of the buttocks are the largest muscles in your body. They make up the gluteus maximus. 'Maximus' means biggest in Latin. 'Gluteus' comes from a Greek word for rump or behind. These muscles support your upper body as you walk. They also allow you to turn and swivel your hips.

A protective shell

Why do we have this basin of bone? It contains several important parts of the body which need support and protection. The body's waste system is in the pelvis. When you eat and drink, the body gets rid of the things it does not need. Waste water passes into the bladder. The bladder is a bag which can stretch. A strong muscle keeps the bag closed. When the muscle loosens, muscles in the wall of the bladder tighten. This squeezes the waste water out. Solid waste passes down a long tube in the pelvis. Muscles in the tube force the solid waste out of the body.

A woman's pelvis is wider than a man's. This makes room for the **uterus**. It also gives extra protection. The uterus is the part of a woman's body where a baby grows. When the baby is ready to be born, the very strong muscles which make up the uterus begin to push the baby out. Women need these very strong muscles in the pelvis to give birth. The muscles squeeze and tighten. They work for hours.

▼ These women are expecting babies. They are doing exercises to strengthen the muscles of the pelvis. This will make them strong and fit when they give birth.

The arms and legs

▼ Some of the bones in our arms and legs are big and strong. Others are small and delicate. Our arms and legs are used to move around, to defend ourselves, to fetch and carry, and to make things.

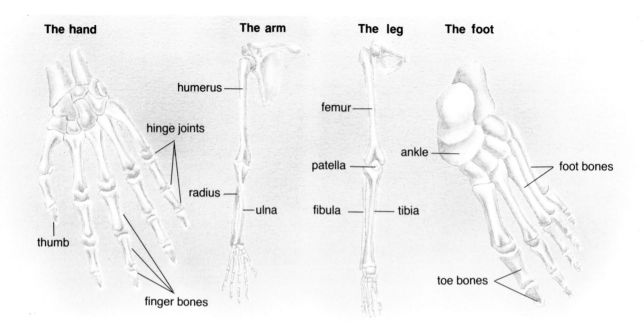

The hand

thumb

finger bones

hinge joints

The arm

humerus

radius

ulna

The leg

femur

patella

fibula — tibia

The foot

ankle

foot bones

toe bones

◄ Our hands are very strong, but they can also carry out very delicate tasks. This Chinese man is drawing out letters with both hands. He has fine control of the ink brushes.

The arm has three bones between the shoulder and the wrist. There is one bone in the top half. This bone between the shoulder and the elbow is called the **humerus**. There are two thinner bones between the elbow and the wrist. These are the **radius** and the **ulna**. They are joined to the humerus by a hinge joint at the elbow. Strong muscles raise and lower the arm. Muscles below the elbow control movement of the lower arm and the wrist.

Three sets of nerves run from the spinal cord, along the shoulder and down the arms. Have you ever banged the 'funny

▶ Ballet dancers must train every day. They develop very strong muscles in their thighs, calves and feet. They learn to balance on the tips of their toes.

bone' in your elbow? You feel a pain shoot down your arm. The funny bone is not really a bone at all. It is a nerve at the end of your humerus. It got its name from the humerus. Humerus sounds like the word humorous, which means funny.

The bones in the wrists and hands are small and delicate. Look at your hand. The fingers are hinged in three places, so you can grip things. You have a thumb set lower than the fingers. It can bend towards the hand. The thumb makes the hand work better. Only humans, apes and monkeys have hands like this.

On foot

The bones of the leg are like the bones in the arm, but they are bigger. One long bone runs from the pelvis to the knee. This thigh bone is the femur. There is a hinge joint at the knee. Two thinner bones run

from the knee to the ankle. One is the **tibia**. The other is much thinner and is called the **fibula**. The knee takes a lot of strain. It is protected by a heart-shaped bone called the kneecap or **patella**. The patella fits into a deep groove at the botton of the femur. It is held in place by strong ligaments.

The leg muscles have to be strong. We use them all the time for walking and running. The thigh muscles raise and lower the leg. The muscles in the lower leg control the movement of the ankles, feet and toes. The **Achilles' tendon** joins these muscles to the heel.

There are lots of small bones in the ankles and feet. Many joints in the foot move so that you can walk along. The feet support the whole body. They are shaped so that you can stand up straight without toppling over.

Growing bones

A baby's bones are made of cartilage. They are quite soft. The bones get harder as the child grows older. Bones grow with the child. A new-born baby is about 50 centimetres long. An adult is usually more than three times that height. As the bones grow, stores of calcium phosphate build up. These stores are kept in the bones until they are needed. Then the blood takes them round the body.

Damaged bones

Bones can be broken in accidents, playing games or in a fall. A baby's soft bones don't often break. Bones become thinner and more brittle as a person gets old. An old person's bones break more easily. A break in a bone is called a **fracture**. There are different kinds of fractures. When a bone breaks but does not push through the skin it is called a simple fracture. If the broken bone pushes out through the skin it is called a compound fracture. Broken bones might damage soft parts inside the body. A broken rib could hurt the heart or lungs. A fractured skull could cause brain damage.

◀ A broken bone has to be set, or held in the proper position, if it is to grow together correctly. A plaster cast keeps the bone rigid.

► **Bone cells are light and strong. They multiply to form new bone for growth and repair.**

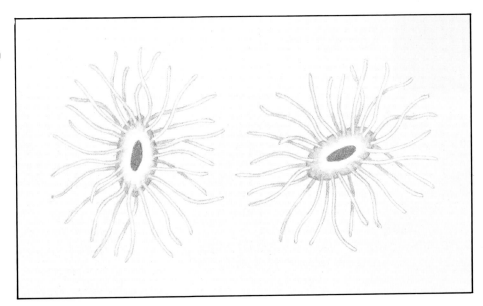

Broken bones heal by growing together again. Blood hardens and covers the broken edges of the bone. **Minerals** are the substances that make bones hard. The minerals seep out of broken bones. The broken bones become soft without the minerals. New bone called **callus** slowly closes the gap in the bone. The callus hardens and the bone is back to normal.

Bones heal themselves, but they still need some help. If you break your leg and just leave it to heal, the bone might not mend straight. The jagged ends of bone would dig into the body cells round the fracture. This would be very painful. A doctor will set your leg in plaster. This keeps the leg rigid. The broken bone cannot move. The ends are held together inside the plaster cast. They will grow together properly and will not damage other parts of your leg.

Broken bones do not always mend inside a plaster cast. Sometimes the muscles around the fracture are so strong they pull the bones apart again. This can happen to the bone in the upper leg where the muscles are very strong. A weight is used to pull against the muscles so that the broken ends stay together. This is called **traction**.

How a broken bone heals

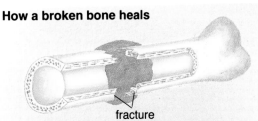

1   The blood around the break hardens and covers the broken ends of bone.

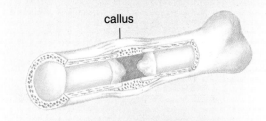

2   Minerals are taken into the bloodstream. The ends of the bone are soft. Callus starts to grow from the broken ends.

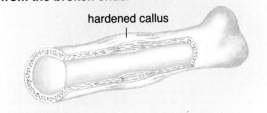

3   The callus joins together the broken ends of bone. Then it begins to harden. When it has hardened completely, the broken limb can be used again.

27

Unable to move

There are other kinds of injuries to bones and muscles besides fractures. Most of these injuries are very painful. It is often hard to move around. One type of injury is a **sprain**. A sprain occurs when muscles or ligaments are strained or torn. Another type of injury is a **dislocation**. A dislocation happens when a bone slips out of its joint. It usually takes a great deal of force to make this happen. Doctors can usually push the bone back into place, but the joint usually hurts for some time. A disc is a name for the pad of cartilage between each bone of the spine. Sometimes a disc can move out of place and press on the spinal cord. This is called a slipped disc and is very painful.

Bones and joints

If body cells are harmed, or have a disease, they can become hot and painful. This pain is called **inflammation**. Bones can become inflamed on the surface or inside. A person with inflamed bone marrow has a high fever and is in great pain. Another bone disease is caused by lack of a mineral called **calcium**. A low supply of calcium makes the bones thin and brittle. Then, they break very easily.

▼ Injuries to bones or muscles may stop us moving around for quite some time. This boy is being given traction for a broken leg. The leg is held rigid while a weight attached to cords pulls against the muscles.

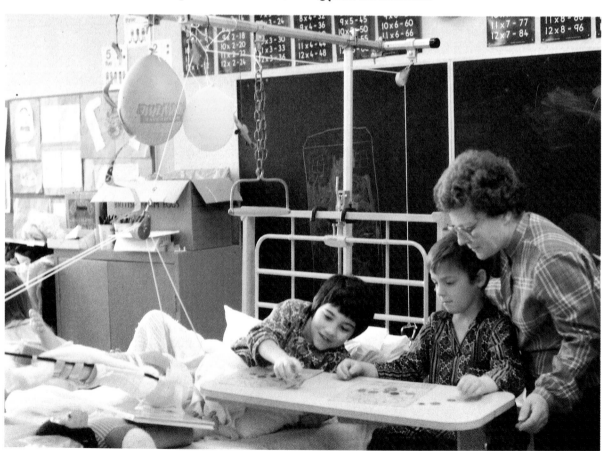

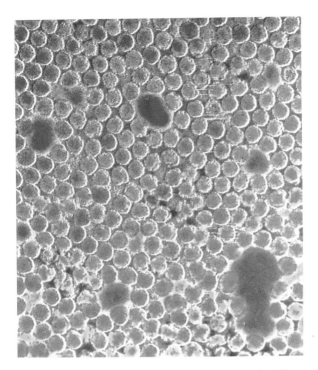

▲ This picture shows the polio virus. It goes into the body and goes into the cells in the spinal cord. There, it multiplies. People who catch polio may suffer paralysis.

▲ When we are no longer able to support our own bodies, a stick or walking frame helps us get around. Many people with arthritis need to walk in this way.

Joints can become inflamed too. This disease is called **arthritis**. It may happen because the membranes produce too much fluid. This makes the joints swell and become painful. Some people with this disease have knobbly joints. This is because the cartilage has worn away and the bones are rubbing together. The ends of the bones thicken and stick out.

Nerves and muscles

A damaged nerve cannot send messages to a muscle. A muscle cannot work on its own. Damage to the nerves or muscles can stop the muscles working. The damage causes **paralysis**. Polio is a serious disease of the nerves in the spine. It is caused by tiny living things called **viruses**. Viruses can only grow inside a cell. They damage the cell and then move on to other cells. If the nerve cells are destroyed, the person may never be able to move again. People can be protected against diseases like polio. The body can produce a substance to fight viruses. Doctors can give the body a tiny amount of the virus. This is called **vaccination**. The body has time to make the substance to fight the disease. This substance stays in the body and protects it in the future.

If supplies of blood to the brain are cut off, the brain will become damaged. It stops sending messages along the spinal cord. The person then suffers a stroke. A stroke can leave the person paralysed down one side of the body. Multiple sclerosis is a serious disease which hardens the coverings of the nerves in the brain or spinal cord. People who have multiple sclerosis slowly lose the use of their muscles.

In the hospital

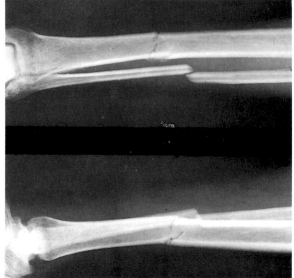

▼ This child is having an X-ray. The X-ray picture allows doctors to see inside the leg. They can tell how badly the leg is broken. They can see how to set the bones so that the leg heals properly.

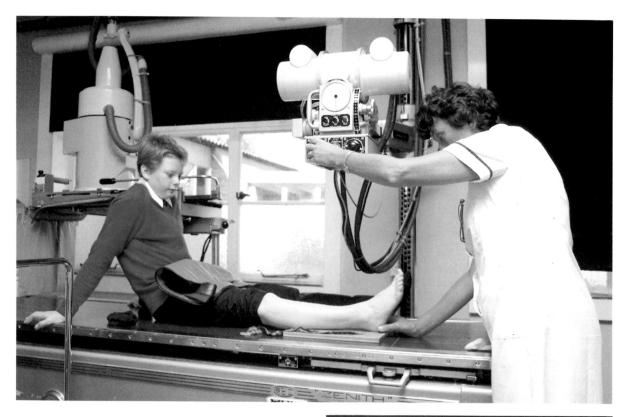

If you break a bone, you may have to go to hospital to have it set. Suppose you have broken your leg. What happens at the hospital?

The doctor needs to know where the bone is broken and what the fracture looks like. The doctor cannot see inside your leg. A hospital worker takes a special picture of your leg. This is called an **X-ray**. You lie on a bed and a camera is held over the place where the bone is broken. X-rays are a type of ray which we cannot see. The light of the X-ray can look right through the skin to the bones inside. The picture does not show any muscles, nerves or blood. It just shows the bones very clearly.

Mending the body

If the break is a simple fracture, your leg is set in plaster. Sometimes it is not as easy as this. Some broken bones have to be screwed or pinned to keep them in place. If the bone is smashed into many pieces, the doctor has to cut the body open to pin the bone together.

Operations on bones are carried out by very skilled doctors. They are called **orthopaedic surgeons**. They take care not to damage other parts of the body round the bone. The work may take many hours.

Doctors and nurses work together as a team.

Sometimes a leg or arm is so badly damaged that it has to be cut off altogether. This is called **amputation**.

Healthy bone marrow makes about 175 thousand million new **red blood cells** a day. We would die without red blood cells. Sometimes a person's bone marrow stops making red blood cells. Surgeons may be able to replace the marrow with marrow from someone else. This is called a bone marrow **transplant**.

▶ Surgeons are very skilled at mending parts of the body. During an operation, everything must be kept free from germs. The instruments, clothes and whole room must be spotlessly clean.

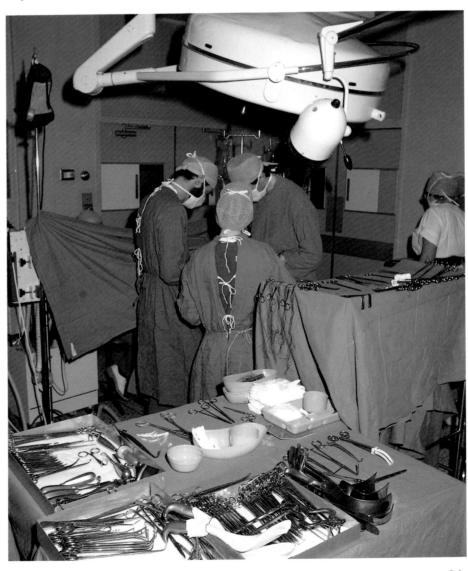

◀ An X-ray picture looks rather like the negative of a normal photograph, except that it is much larger. This picture shows a leg that has a fractured tibia and fibula.

Made to measure

▼ This device has been made to help the patient use his hands, which are twisted and bent.

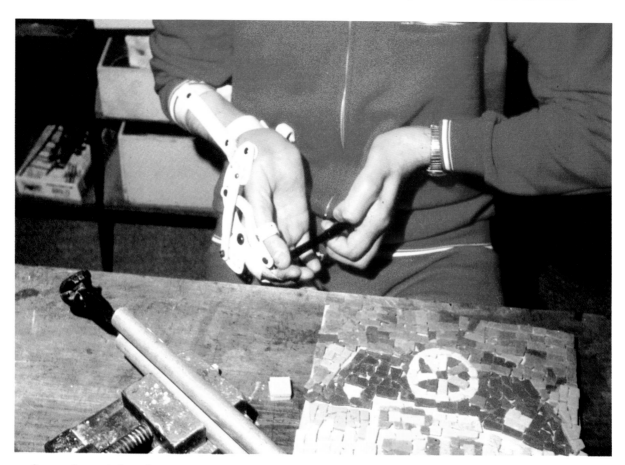

Sometimes joints become so painful that it is difficult to move them. Nowadays, people can be given new joints. Many older people have new hip joints. The old bone is cut away and a new ball-and-socket joint is put in its place. The new joints are usually made of a type of plastic. Doctors try to make these new joints very like the real bones inside our bodies. In time, the ligaments and muscles build up round the new joint and hold it firmly in place. Knee joints can be replaced in the same way. After a day or two the patient can walk about. Exercise helps to build up the muscles but the patient must be careful not to twist the new joint out of place.

New arms and legs

Someone who has an arm or a leg amputated can be given a new one that has been specially made. These **artificial limbs** have been used for hundreds of years. Early ones were made by copying suits of armour. They could bend at the joints but they were stiff and heavy. Now artificial limbs are made of wood, leather, metal or plastic. They can move very much like a real limb.

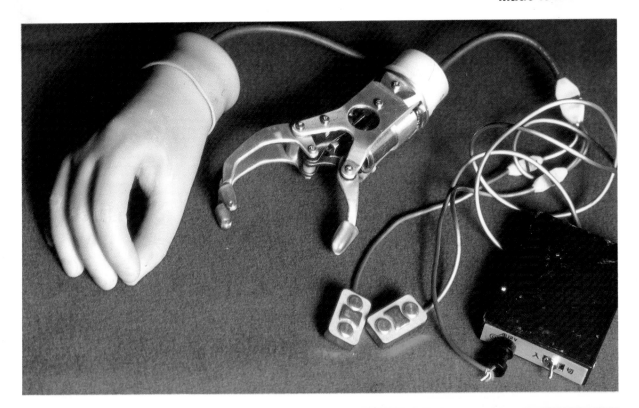

▲ The first artificial hands were uncomfortable to wear and clumsy to use. Today, engineers can use electronics and plastics to make hands which can pick up objects and hold them quite easily.

► Learning to use an artificial leg can be a painful and slow process. Once the body has become used to the new leg, however, quite hard exercise is possible. This woman is able to play tennis.

Suppose someone has a whole leg removed. They can be given an artificial leg instead. The artificial leg will have a hip joint, knee joint and an ankle joint. The artificial leg weighs about half as much as the real leg and is fixed on firmly with straps.

There are no nerves or muscles in an artificial leg. The patient has to learn to walk in a new way. The muscles in the upper part of the body are used to swing the new leg forward. It may take two or three months to learn to walk with an artificial leg.

Getting around

Disabled people cannot use some part of their body properly. They may be deaf or blind, or they may not be able to use their legs or their arms. People may be born with a disability. An accident or an illness like polio may damage part of the body. Disabled people are affected in different ways.

Some disabled people can only get around in wheelchairs or in special cars. Look around the town you live in and try to imagine what this means.

Everyday living

How can you go up and down steps or through a narrow doorway in a wheelchair? Many problems like these can be solved.

Shopping centres and all other buildings which people need to visit can have ramps as well as steps. Offices and shops often have lifts. Someone in a wheelchair can only use a lift if the buttons are low enough for them to reach. Doorways, paths and passages can be made wide enough for wheelchairs. Disabled people need parking places near shops. Public toilets should be easy for them to get into and to use.

▼ Cars can be specially adapted for disabled people. Some can be controlled with the hands only. Some can be made with room for a wheelchair.

▶ This kitchen has been built so that everything can be reached from a wheelchair. The cooker and sink are at just the right height. The cupboards are at ground level.

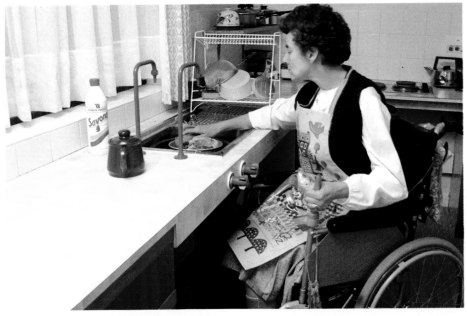

▼ These disabled people in California, USA, are taking part in a wheelchair race. They need strong arm muscles to cover the 1500 metre course.

On the move again

If you are ill in bed, you do not use your muscles much. If you are ill for a long time, the muscles become weak. The same thing happens if you break an arm or a leg and cannot use it for several weeks, or even months. When you are well enough to move around again, the muscles will not work properly. They have become thinner and weak. The joints are stiff and hard to move. You need some help to strengthen the muscles again.

Exercise helps to build the weak muscles up again. The muscles may feel stiff. The blood is not bringing enough oxygen to them, so that they cannot move smoothly or for long. Pushing and rubbing the muscles hard with the fingers gets the blood flowing smoothly. This is called **massage**. Sometimes bones and joints are slightly out of place. They can be eased back into place by **manipulation**. A trained person can push and pull the bones or joints gently until they slip back into the right place.

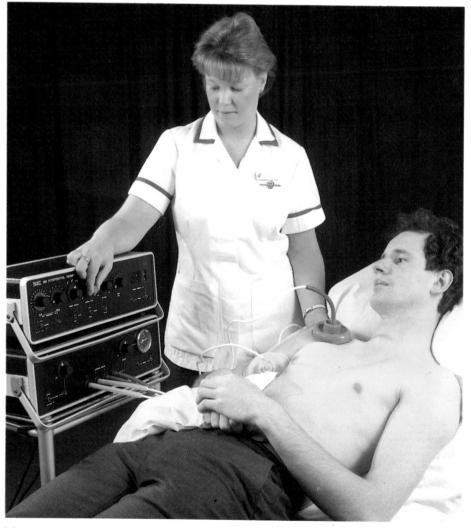

◄ Both hands and machines can be used to help the body get moving again. This patient has had pads placed on his chest and arm. These are connected to a machine which will help him to recover faster.

Feeling better

If you need this type of treatment, you can go to a **physiotherapist**. Many physiotherapists work in hospitals. They treat muscles and bones from the outside. They help patients who are staying in hospital and patients who come to the hospital just for special treatment. The patient's doctor writes notes to tell the physiotherapist what is wrong. The physiotherapist chooses the best exercises to strengthen the patient's muscles.

There are other ways of healing pain caused by nerves and bones. **Chiropractors** use their hands to move the parts of the spine. They work on the nerves, which hurt if they get caught in the wrong place. The name chiropractor comes from the Greek words for using the hands.

Osteopaths heal problems by the movement of bones. Osteopaths use massage and manipulation to put bones back into the right place.

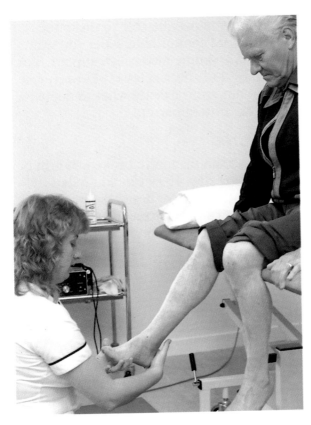

▲ A physiotherapist checks the movement of a patient's ankle.

▶ A swimming pool is the ideal place for the physiotherapist and her patients. The water holds the body up. The limbs do not feel so heavy. This makes it easier to move the muscles and joints.

First aid

You may see someone injured in a road accident, or fall and break a bone. What should you do? The main thing is to keep calm. Do not panic. Call an adult if you can. If there is no one around, telephone for help. Call an ambulance to take the person to hospital. If you know some first aid rules, you may be able to make the person more comfortable while you wait. First aid is simple medical treatment. You can learn it at special classes. However, if you do not know exactly what to do **never** touch an injured person.

Fractures

The person may have broken an arm or a leg or some ribs. How can you tell? First, the person may have heard the bone crack. He or she will be in pain and will find it difficult to move the broken part. Do not

Tying a sling

knot

safety pin

◄ Slide a triangular bandage under the arm and up to the shoulder. Put a soft pad between the arm and chest. Bring the back point of the triangle round the person's neck and tie it to the other point above the collar-bone. Bring the third point round the elbow and pin it to the front of the bandage. You can make an emergency sling from a belt or scarf, or tuck the arm into a buttoned-up jacket or cardigan.

let them try to move. Broken bones can do more damage by moving. There may be swelling around the broken bone. The bone may even be poking through the skin.

Do not move the person. Make sure the person does not use the injured body part. **Never** remove a motor-cyclist's helmet, in case the skull is fractured. Pieces of bone may be pressed into the brain if you do. You may have to wait a while for help. Try to keep the person warm. If you have a coat or a blanket, put it over the injured person.

Sprains

Sometimes an injured person may have a sprained ankle or wrist. This is very painful. The ankle or wrist will be bruised and swollen. The first thing to do to help is to reduce the swelling. You do this by putting something cold on the sprain. Soak a pad of cloth in cold water and put it gently on the swollen area. Do not press on the injured part of the body. A person who has been trained may put on a firm bandage. It will hold the joint in place while the ligaments and muscles mend.

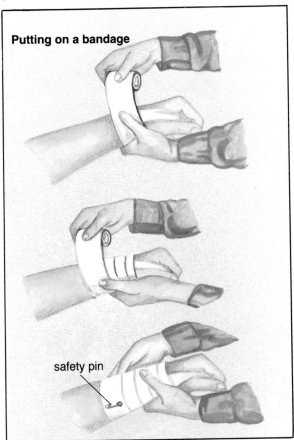

Putting on a bandage

safety pin

▲ A bandage can be used to support a sprained ankle or wrist, or to hold a dressing in place. The bandage is wound round and round the injured part. Each layer partly overlaps the layer before. You start bandaging at the bottom of the injured part and work your way upwards. The end of the bandage should be turned in and fixed with a safety pin.

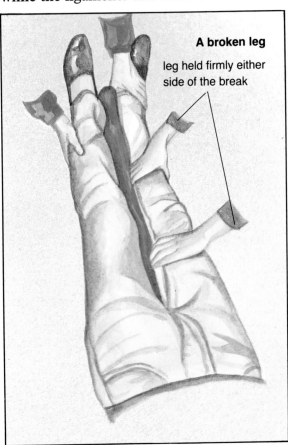

A broken leg

leg held firmly either side of the break

▲ If someone has broken a leg, the leg may be bent or lying at an awkward angle. There may even be an open wound. The first thing to do is to call an ambulance. The leg can be supported but not moved. Place one hand over the leg above the break and one hand below the break. Then, blankets, cushions or coats can be wedged around the leg to add extra support.

Body fuel

Your body is like a machine. Machines cannot work without fuel. Some machines burn oil or coal. The fuels we 'burn' are oxygen and food. They give us the energy to move. Energy makes all the parts of our bodies work.

How do we use food? When you eat a meal, your body breaks the food down. Then your blood carries it to different parts of your body. Food is made up of different **nutrients**. These do different jobs. **Proteins** give energy, but they also build up cells. You need a lot of protein while you are growing. Meat, fish, some vegetables, cheese and other dairy foods all contain protein. **Carbohydrates** give the most energy. They are found in sugar and starchy foods such as bread and potatoes.

▲ When a little boy, called Eric, eats bananas he changes into the cartoon character of Bananaman. He becomes amazingly strong. Fruit and vegetables contain vitamins and minerals to help keep you strong and healthy, although maybe not quite as strong as Bananaman!

◀ Milk contains calcium which strengthens bones and teeth. Children need plenty of calcium because their bones are still growing.

▲ People in some parts of the world often do not have enough to eat. Sometimes there is no rain, so their crops will not grow. This hungry family in Africa is waiting for a plane to arrive with food supplies.

Fats also provide energy. They make part of your cells too, and keep you warm. Butter, cream, milk, cheese and nuts are fatty foods.

Vitamins do not give energy but they are very important for good health. Vitamin D builds strong bones and teeth. It is contained in green vegetables, and made by sunlight. Bones also need minerals such as calcium and **phosphorus** which are found in milk. **Iron** can be found in green vegetables, fish and meat.

What should we eat?

It is important to eat the right mixture of nutrients. People who do not eat the right foods are not healthy. Their muscles become weak. Their bones may become deformed. Children who do not eat enough vitamin D may suffer from rickets. This means their bones become soft and their legs bend outwards. Lack of calcium weakens bones and teeth and makes them break easily.

Nutrients are stored in the body for several days. The only one which is not stored is vitamin C. You must eat foods containing vitamin C every day. These include fresh vegetables and fruit, particularly oranges or grapefruit.

Keeping fit

You need exercise to keep your body fit. Muscles use oxygen. When you breathe, oxygen goes into your lungs. The heart pumps it round in the blood. Exercise strengthens the heart and the lungs. It also strengthens other muscles in your body. Muscles work better when they are strong. Joints are not stiff if they are used a lot.

Jogging, cycling, brisk walking and skipping make you breathe harder to draw in more oxygen. These activities are all **aerobic** exercises. Aerobic means 'with air'. As you get fitter, you can keep doing the exercises for longer. Other types of exercise need a fast burst of energy. They are **anaerobic** exercises. In anaerobic exercise the lungs cannot draw oxygen in quickly enough, so the muscles use up the energy that is stored within them. The muscles can work very quickly but they cannot keep it up for long. Anaerobic exercise strengthens the muscles. Weight-training is anaerobic. So is a fast sprint. At the end you puff and pant to get more oxygen. If the muscles do not get oxygen they tighten. This sudden movement of a muscle hurts. It is called **cramp**.

▲ Some people like to build up their muscles until they are huge. They train every day. You do not need to be a muscle man or woman to be fit. Regular, gentle exercise will keep you healthy and looking more natural.

▶ A long race is aerobic exercise. The runners keep up an even pace and breathe in oxygen for the muscles to use. The final sprint is anaerobic. The runners use stored muscle energy.

Easy does it

The best all-round exercise is swimming. It strengthens the heart and lungs, strengthens the muscles and keeps the joints supple. Bending and stretching exercises prevent stiff joints. They are very good for the spine. Stretching is also good for the muscles. Some people prefer to do an aerobic exercise such as jogging or cycling, as well as an anaerobic one, such as weight-training.

Most children get enough exercise when they play games. Adults need to exercise regularly two or three times a week. They must be careful not to do too much at once, especially if they are not used to exercise. Exercise must be planned. If you start hard exercise when your muscles are cold, you may strain or tear them. Doing some stretching exercises first warms up the muscles. Bending and stretching after the exercise allows the muscles to cool down and helps them relax again.

▼ Look carefully at the chart. It shows how different kinds of sport help you to fitness in different ways. Compare the sports with each other. Which do you think is best for you?

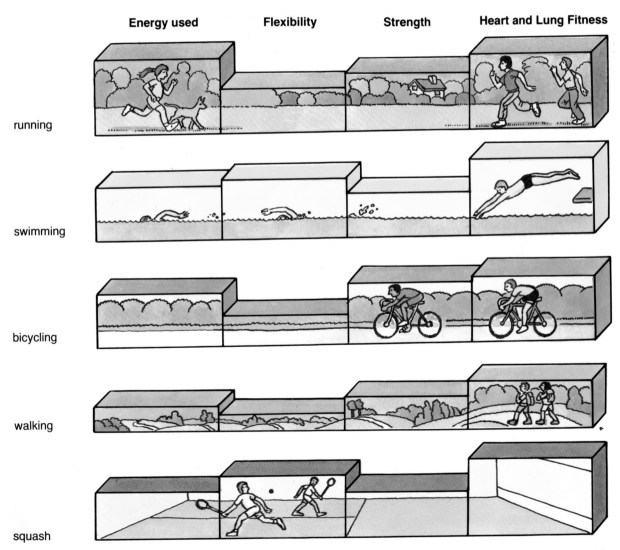

A changing world

The first people on the Earth did not have all the things we have today. They had to hunt for their food. The bones and muscles of their bodies developed so that they could run fast, walk long distances, throw stones and spears, and carry heavy objects. They had to be strong.

Our bodies are still the same but our lives have changed. Today, many people spend their lives sitting down. They get into a car or a train which takes them to work. Then they sit at an office desk all day. In the evening, they sit down and watch television. They often eat foods which have been prepared in a factory. These foods do not have the nutrients of fresh food.

People who live like this will not stay healthy. Our bodies were designed for action. We need exercise and good food. People who have to sit down all day could try walking to work or taking some exercise in the evenings or at weekends. Playing squash or jogging round the block would strengthen their muscles!

▼ A South American Indian takes aim with his bow and arrow. Our bodies were designed for a hunter's life, not for sitting in chairs all day.

New bodies

Will our bodies change in the future? They might not change much while we live on the Earth, but what will happen if we spend more and more time in space? We are kept on the Earth by **gravity**. This is a force which pulls everything towards the centre of the Earth. It gives us weight. If there was no gravity we would be weightless. We would float away.

There is no gravity in space. You have probably seen pictures of people in space floating around in their spaceships. Studies have been made into the effects of weightlessness. On Earth, our skeletons support our bodies and keep our feet on the ground. We would not need the same sort of skeleton if we spent all our time floating in space. Perhaps we would develop bodies with a skeleton on the outside, like a crab, or lose our skeletons completely!

▲ One hundred years ago, most people walked to work. Today we use escalators, lifts, trains and cars. In order to keep fit, we must take regular exercise.

► Some astronauts have spent long periods in weightless conditions. It has been found that their bones begin to lose calcium. Unless they take in extra calcium, their bones become brittle.

Glossary

Achilles tendon: a group of strong fibres which attach the muscle at the back of the lower leg to the heel

aerobic: using oxygen. In aerobic exercise the lungs work harder to take in more oxygen

amputation: to cut off a limb, especially an arm or a leg

anaerobic: without using oxygen. Anaerobic exercise does not use oxygen for energy. It uses energy already stored in the muscles

anatomy: the study of the structure of the human body

arthritis: inflammation of a joint. Arthritis is found in the joints of people suffering from diseases such as gout and rheumatism

artificial limb: an arm, a leg, a foot or a hand that has been made in a factory. Artificial limbs are used to replace limbs that have had to be cut off or have been lost in accidents

ball-and-socket joint: a joint made by a round knob moving freely in a cup-shaped holder. It allows movement in all directions

brain: the 'computer' in our heads which controls everything we do

brain stem: the beginning of the spinal cord at the base of the brain

calcium: a substance which we need for strong bones, teeth and healthy muscles. Calcium is found in milk

calcium phosphate: a substance made of calcium and phosphorous which the blood carries to the bone cells. It makes the bones hard and strong

callus: the material which forms while a break in a bone heals

carbohydrate: an energy-giving substance found in foods such as potatoes and bread

cartilage: a tough, rubbery material which protects the ends of bones. It makes your outer ear, nose and windpipe

cell: a very small part or unit. All living things are made up of cells

chiropractor: a person who believes that many illnesses are caused by nerves in the spine being under pressure. A chiropractor works to move the bones slightly to release the pressure

cramp: a sudden pain caused when muscles suddenly contract, or shorten

cranium: the bones of the head that protect the brain

diaphragm: the large flat muscle in the body that separates the chest from the stomach and makes the lungs work

dislocation: an injury caused by one of the bones in a joint slipping out of place

energy: the power to do work. People get energy from food. Engines get energy from petrol

fat: an energy-giving substance found in foods such as butter, cream, cheese and meat

femur: the largest bone in the body. It is found in the top half of your leg, above the knee

fibrous joint: a joint in which the bones are fixed firmly together by strong fibres which allow little or no movement

fibula: the thin bone found at the back of the leg below the knee

fracture: a break in a bone

gliding joint: a joint where two flat surfaces move over one another. The joints at the wrists are gliding joints

glucose: a simple sugar which many living things use to give them energy

gravity: the force which pulls something towards the centre of the Earth. If you throw a ball in the air, gravity makes it fall back to the ground

grey matter: a substance in the brain and the centre of the spinal cord, where nerves bring messages from the body and take back instructions to the muscles

hard palate: the hard 'roof' of your mouth. The hard palate is made of bone

hinge joint: a joint where movement is only backwards and forwards, like a door. The elbow is a hinge joint

humerus: the bone in the arm between the shoulder and the elbow

inflammation: the way body tissues react to infection or injury. They become hot, tender, swollen and painful

invertebrate: any animal which has no backbone. All animals are either invertebrates or vertebrates

involuntary: something which happens automatically, without thought

iron: a mineral found in green vegetables, fish and meat. It is needed for healthy blood

ligament: a strip of a strong rubbery material which hold the two bones of a joint together

manipulation: to handle or move with the hands. Manipulation of parts of the body is used sometimes to ease pain and stiffness

marrow: the soft, fatty substance in the middle of bones where blood cells are made

massage: pushing and rubbing the muscles and joints of the body to improve the blood flow and ease pain and stiffness

membrane: a thin lining or covering

mineral: any natural substance found in the ground which is not formed from plant or animal life. Our bodies get the minerals they need from food to help build healthy bones and teeth

muscle: a type of material in the body which can shorten itself to produce movement

nerve: part of a network of tiny 'cables' which pass messages from all parts of the body to the brain, and back again

nervous system: the system which controls all movements and feelings by carrying messages between the brain and all parts of the body

neuron: a nerve cell. A neuron is the basic unit of the nervous system

nutrient: a nourishing ingredient in food

orthopaedic surgeon: a doctor who cures illness by operating on part of the skeleton

osteopath: a person who believes that many illnesses are caused by misplacement of the bones. Osteopaths massage the muscles and adjust the bones to correct this

paralysis: loss of movement or feeling

patella: the cap-like bone that covers the front of the knee joint. Also called the kneecap

pelvis: the part of the body at the top of the legs which is formed by the two hip bones

phosphorus: a substance found in all living things. We need it for strong bones and healthy cells

physiotherapist: someone who treats muscles and bones by using heat, massage, manipulation, or exercises

pivot joint: a joint where one bone twists against another. The pivot joint in your neck lets you move your head up or down and from side-to-side

protein: an energy-giving substance found in foods such as meat, fish, cheese, eggs and beans

radius: the outer bone in the lower arm which lies between the elbow and the thumb

red blood cell: a part of the blood which carries oxygen

rib: one of the bones in your chest. The ribs protect your heart and lungs

skeleton: the framework of bones or shell which supports the body of a person or animal

skull: the bones which make up the head of an animal. The skull protects the brain, eyes and ears of an animal

spinal cord: the string of fibres which runs down the inside of the spine. The spinal cord takes messages between the brain and all other parts of the body

spine: the line of small bones that runs down the length of the back of all vertebrates. It is also called the backbone

sprain: the injury of a joint damages muscles, ligaments and tendons

sternum: the long flat bone which is found down the centre of the chest, between the two sides of your rib-cage. It is also called the breastbone

stirrup: one of the three tiny bones inside the ear. It looks like the stirrup used on a saddle

tendon: a band of string or a tough, rubbery material which joins the muscles to bones in the body

thorax: the middle part of the body, between the neck and the stomach. The heart and lungs are found in the thorax

tibia: the shin bone, found at the front of the leg below the knee

traction: the act of pulling. Weights are used to pull muscles and keep broken bones in place

transplant: to remove a damaged part of the body and replace it with a healthy part from another person

ulna: the inner bone of the arm which leads from the elbow towards the little finger side of the wrist

uterus: the part of the body in a female human or other mammal in which babies grow

vaccination: specially treated germs which are injected into the body, so that the body can learn how to protect itself against them. The body will then be protected against the illness in the future

vertebrae: the line of small bones found down the centre of the back in vertebrates

vertebrate: any animal with a bony skeleton and a backbone. Fish, amphibians, reptiles, birds and mammals are all vertebrates

virus: a kind of germ. Viruses cause disease when they get inside the body's cells. Mumps and flu are both caused by viruses

vitamin: a substance which is found in foods such as vegetables and fruit. Tiny amounts of vitamins are needed for good health and growth

voluntary: something which does not happen automatically, but is controlled by thought

white matter: a substance in the outer layer of the spinal cord which carries messages to and from the brain

X-ray: a light ray which can be used to photograph some parts of the body from the outside

Index